KAYAKING

ADVENTURE SPORTS

KAYAKING

SCOTT WURDINGER & LESLIE RAPPARLIE

CREATIVE EDUCATION

Published by Creative Education
123 South Broad Street, Mankato, Minnesota 56001
Creative Education is an imprint of the The Creative
Company

Design and production by Blue Design
(www.bluedes.com)
Art direction by Rita Marshall

Photographs by Alamy (Alaska Stock LLC, Bill
Bachmann, Steve Bardens, Buzz Pictures, Chris A
Crumley, Danita Delimont, Robert Destefano, Harold
R. Stinnette Photo Stock, Chris Howes / Wild Place
Photography, Andre Jenny, steve mcalister, Ron
Niebrugge, Barrie Rokeach, Stephen Frink Collection,
Stock Connection, David Wall, Westend61),
SportsChrome (BONGARTS, Brian Drake, Sport the
Library, Kim Stallknecht), LYNN SELDON

Printed in the United States of America

Library of Congress Cataloging-in-Publication Data

Wurdinger, Scott D.
Kayaking / by Scott Wurdinger and Leslie Rapparlie.
p. cm. — (Adventure sports)
Includes bibliographical references and index.
ISBN-13 : 978-1-58341-397-5
1. Kayaking—Juvenile literature. I. Wurdinger, Scott D.
II. Adventure sports (Mankato, Minn.)

GV784.3.W87 2006
797.122'4—dc22   2005051057

First edition

9 8 7 6 5 4 3 2 1

KAYAKING

In the distance, the sound of crashing water and wild rapids resonates through the air. Powerful water tumbles over smooth rocks, reverberating like a jet airplane engine jumping to a steady purr. Around a long, lazy bend they appear—dozens of white, breaking waves crashing in chaotic directions. Like a gymnast, the water jumps, dives, and rolls every which way. As a lone kayaker approaches the rushing rapids, anxiety and excitement grow more intense. The purr of colliding waves rises to a deep and heavy roar. Soon enough, the thrashing water is just a paddle stroke away. The water quickly picks up speed, forcing anything afloat toward the treacherous rapids below.

The kayaker's eyes dart from left to right, scouting the length of river in sight. Paddling with quick, careful movements, the kayaker navigates

Paddling in a kayak is like no other boat ride. Navigating curvy rivers, facing roaring rapids, dodging boulders and unseen rocks—these are just a few of the elements of this adventurous sport combining skill and courage.

Kayaking offers people of all ages a chance to relax or play on the water. From leisurely drifting down a peaceful river, to attacking large rapids, to exploring unknown ocean coves, kayakers can choose their own kind of excitement.

around boulders and obstacles in the water. The boat dips and swerves, water spilling over the bow. The paddler's breath is rhythmic and steady as the water becomes his sole focus of concentration. As quickly as it began, it is over. The paddler floats once again on a serene section of river, the sound of crashing water fading into the distance.

"There is magic in the feel of a paddle . . . a magic compounded of distance, adventure, solitude, and peace," wrote American conservationist Sigurd Olson. It is this magic that leads kayakers of all skill levels, in all parts of the world, to the water. Some live for the thrill of speeding through rough white-water rapids, while others prefer the relaxation of an afternoon paddle around a remote lake. Still others thrive on the adrenaline rush of flipping their boat on a rising ocean wave. All kayakers though, have one thing in common: a passion for the adventure of their sport. It's what leads them to dip their boat into the water time and time again.

An Old Vessel

Sleek vessels able to glide quietly through the water, kayaks were first used by natives of the far north to hunt animals such as seals, walruses, and whales. In fact, the word "kayak" means "hunter's boat." Archaeologists have evidence indicating that kayaks were first built between 4,000 and 6,000 years ago by people who ranged across the Arctic from the Aleutian Islands to Greenland, including parts of Siberia, the Bering Strait, and northern Canada.

These people of the North collected driftwood from beaches and constructed it into kayak frames using primitive tools made from antler, ivory, or bone. They generally carved the frames from fir, pine, spruce, or willow. In order to keep water out of the kayak, the top was usually covered with seal, sea lion, caribou, or walrus skins.

The first kayaks proved to be reliable hunting vessels, and for centuries after its invention, the kayak remained relatively unchanged. However, over the past 100 years or so, the materials from which kayaks are constructed have changed dramatically. As public interest in wilderness exploration and travel grew in the late 19th and early 20th centuries, wooden kayaks gave way to folding kayaks.

The ability to cut through water silently made kayaks ideal for hunting prey. Long ago, some hunters stalked sea animals such as sea lions and seals by covering the front of their kayak with white cloth to appear as a drifting iceberg.

Plastic is the most durable and popular material used for white-water rapid riding. While Kevlar is lighter than plastic, it is used mainly in kayaking competitions, not in exploring rapids and dangerous waterways.

These new, German-built kayaks, made from PVC or hypalon, could fold into a large backpack, allowing individuals to take them on trains to explore distant rivers and lakes.

After 1930, as the use of personal automobiles increased, non-collapsible wood and canvas kayaks were built. These vessels could easily be transported on top of vehicles and saved kayakers the hassle of setting up the boat once they reached the water. Glass-reinforced plastic, also known as fiberglass, became an important material for building kayaks around 1950. Fiberglass allowed companies to mass-produce tougher, lighter kayaks and rendered all previous building materials obsolete.

By the mid-1970s, molded polyethylene became the state-of-the-art material for kayaks, and with its durability and low cost, it remains the most common material used today. Kevlar is another common material for kayaks but has its downfalls. Although Kevlar kayaks weigh up to 20 pounds (9 kg) less than polyethylene kayaks, they are less durable and much more expensive. Still, when compared with the most recently developed material, graphite, Kevlar almost seems cheap. A graphite kayak weighs even less than a Kevlar kayak but costs at least $800 more.

All kayaks are built to glide and offer a smooth, silent ride in the water. The stability and durability of a kayak depends on factors such as material, length, and how high the kayak sits in the water—all of which deserve consideration before one purchases a kayak.

Valdez, Alaska, offers tourists a chance to sea kayak among the seals and sea lions of Prince William Sound. Kayakers can also dodge icebergs as they tour glaciers by kayak on glacial lakes, which are created from melted glacial ice.

Gear for The Adventure

The key to a good kayaking experience is having the right kayak and equipment. Kayaks are designed for specific purposes: long boats for touring; short, narrow ones for racing; and various other shapes and lengths for everything in between. All kayaks are available with single, double, triple, or—in some specialized racing boats—quadruple seats. There are four general classifications of kayaks: recreational, touring, white-water, and freestyle.

Recreational kayaks, generally used for leisurely paddling on flat water, are made of durable polyethylene plastic and have large, open cockpits. Some recreational models are designed to have paddlers sit on top of the boat rather than in it. Sit-on-top kayaks are more comfortable for some people and are easy to climb on again if the kayak tips over. Recreational kayaks are usually 14 feet (4.3 m) long and cost around $300 to $800.

Touring kayaks, which range in size from 14 to 19 feet (4.3–5.8 m), are built for paddling in open water where there might be big waves. These kayaks often have a rudder, which helps keep them moving in a straight line. They also have cargo space, where kayakers can store gear. Touring kayaks are more expensive than other kinds of kayaks, ranging from $1,000 to $2,000.

White-water kayaks are short—generally 6 to 8 feet (1.8–2.4 m)—and wide for stability when running rapids. These kayaks have a lot of rocker, which means that less of the boat is immersed in the water, making the kayak easier to turn and maneuver around rocks and other obstacles. Made of durable polyethylene plastic, white-water kayaks cost around $300 to $800 and can easily withstand the abuse of bashing into and over rocks.

Freestyle kayaks are similar to white-water kayaks, but since they are used for performing tricks, paddlers must be able to spin them even faster than white-water kayaks. The upturned ends of freestyle kayaks provide ample rocker, allowing paddlers to spin, flip, and turn in the water more easily. Freestyle kayaks generally cost a bit more than white-water kayaks, at $600 to $1000.

Like kayaks, paddles come in all shapes and sizes. They are made of a variety of materials, including wood, fiberglass, plastic, aluminum, Kevlar, graphite, and combinations of these materials. Unlike a canoe paddle, a kayak paddle has a blade on either end of the shaft in order to allow for more control in maneuvering.

Kayak paddles can have symmetrical or asymmetrical blades. A symmetrical paddle has blades that face the same direction on both ends, while an asymmetrical paddle has blades that face opposite directions or are at a 90-degree angle to one another. Asymmetrical blades move through the water more easily than symmetrical blades, making them more comfortable for long-distance trips on flat-water. Symmetrical blades move more water at a time but also consume more energy; they are most often used for white-water paddling.

The most common recreational kayak paddle is seven to eight feet (215–240 cm) long, with asymmetrical blades, and may be taken apart in the middle for easy storage. Paddle sizes vary based on the height of the paddler, the size of the paddler's hands, and the size of the kayak being used. Paddle costs generally range from $40 to $440, depending on the material used. Aluminum and plastic paddles are the least expensive and graphite paddles cost the most.

A Personal Flotation Device (PFD), also called a life vest, is an important piece of equipment for all kayakers and, by law, must at least be in the kayak. It is rare to see a kayaker without a PFD on his or her body. United States Coast Guard designated flotation aids (type III vests)—which should be used only in calm water where a rescue can happen quickly—are most commonly used for water sports, such as water skiing, jet skiing, canoeing, and kayaking, in North America. Offshore life jackets (type I vests) and near-shore buoyant vests (type II vests) can be used in fast water where a rescue may take longer due to water conditions or location. These vests, however, can be too bulky for paddling, since they slip over the head and tie around the waist instead of fitting like a shirt around the body. Generally, PFDs must be comfortable so that they do not cause chafing under the arms or on the neck. Vests used in kayaking are typically shorter in length than other boating PFDs so that they do not slide up toward a kayaker's ears while he or she paddles.

When a kayaker is exploring unknown waterways, he or she will often store an extra paddle in the kayak. This is a precaution in case the kayaker encounters rapids or loses the original paddle. The blades of the stored paddle may or may not be the same as those of the primary paddle.

The clothes a kayaker wears are determined by multiple factors. A kayaker should know the water's temperature, extended weather report for the area, and, if sea kayaking, the tide flow; if on a river or lake, the current strength.

A spray skirt is another essential piece of equipment for serious paddlers. Made of a synthetic rubber called neoprene, spray skirts are worn to prevent water from entering the boat in both open and white water, since a kayak filled with water sits lower and is harder to paddle and easier to tip. Often brightly colored, spray skirts are pulled on like a skirt and fit snugly around the paddler's mid-section. They flare out at the bottom so that they can be pulled over the cockpit of the boat. A rubber or elastic cord runs around the edge of most spray skirts and is placed under the lip of the cockpit to create a waterproof seal. Recreational kayakers may not need a spray skirt if they are not concerned with water entering their kayak.

Clothing worn while kayaking can be as casual as a pair of nylon shorts and a t-shirt for the recreational paddler, or as advanced as rubber and neoprene outfits for the hard-core, Arctic paddler. Kayakers must dress according to the type of paddling they will be doing, as well as for weather conditions. In warm weather, paddlers should wear a brimmed hat to protect their neck and face from the sun. Supplex nylon is an excellent material for shirts, pants, and shorts. This material dries much more quickly than cotton, is lightweight, and stays cool in warm conditions.

More sophisticated, layered clothing is necessary when paddling in cold weather. Synthetic long underwear should be worn next to the skin. A second layer, usually a wet suit, provides excellent insulation and keeps the body warm. Wet suits come in a variety of thicknesses, from half a millimeter to seven millimeters (0.02–0.3 in.). The best thickness for kayaking is three millimeters (0.1 in.), which is thick enough to provide good insulation but thin enough to allow adequate flexibility while paddling. The outer layer of clothing, usually a dry suit, keeps heat close to the body and has latex bands that fit snugly around the ankles, wrists, and neck. Hats, gloves, and shoes made of thick neoprene are also available. Wet suits and dry suits can cost hundreds or thousands of dollars depending on the brand and are usually not necessary for recreational paddlers.

Helmets are worn primarily by white-water paddlers, either on rivers or slalom courses, to protect the kayaker's head from rocks and other debris in case the boat tips over. Helmets are not usually necessary when paddling open, calm, or deep water because there is less danger of hitting a rock on the bottom.

Other pieces of equipment used in kayaking include first aid kits, **rescue bags**, flares, radios, and an assortment of camping gear, which can be vital to safety during multi-day kayak trips. The amount and type of equipment a paddler brings will depend on the type of kayaking being done. The recreational paddler might bring only an extra paddle and a water bottle for a short paddle around a lake, whereas an overnight trip across a long stretch of open water may require emergency equipment and camping gear.

Some Alaskan islands can be reached only by boat or airplane. Today, a popular way to visit these islands is by kayak. However, kayakers should be adequately prepared—and experienced—before taking on stretches of open, Arctic water.

The Way Through The Water

Water swishes gently beneath the hull of the kayak as a beginning kayaker raises a paddle to take the first stroke. The blade dips into the water, and the paddler pulls it backward in an attempt to move the kayak forward. Instead of going straight, though, the kayak moves to the left. In order to compensate, the kayaker reaches far to the right with the other side of the paddle and pulls hard through the water. The kayak continues moving to the left. Panicked and frustrated, the paddler continues the same movements, causing the boat to go in a large, uncontrolled circle. Eventually, feeling defeated, the kayaker rests the paddle on top of the kayak and looks to a friend for help.

Beginning kayakers often find learning to steer frustrating, but once they have mastered the various strokes, they quickly become experts at controlling the kayak. The most basic kayaking stroke is the forward one, used to move the kayak in a straight line. To move forward, the kayaker places one blade of the paddle in the water, then pulls the bottom of the paddle toward the body while pushing the top of the paddle away from the body. As the kayaker pulls the paddle through the water, his or her body twists along with it in order to provide stability to the boat and maximum efficiency to the stroke.

The sweep stroke, used to turn the boat, requires a bit more finesse. To execute a sweep stroke, the kayaker leans forward and places the paddle in

Learning to kayak with a friend or family member may lead to a lifetime of enjoying this adventure sport together. Kayaking can also contribute to a stronger and healthier body gained through time spent having fun on the water.

the water near the bow of the boat. Pushing with the top hand and pulling with the bottom hand, the kayaker moves the paddle in a semicircle out toward the stern of the kayak. The kayak turns left when the sweep stroke is done on the right side of the boat and vice versa.

The draw stroke is used to "side-step" the kayak. The paddler places one blade of the paddle in the water an arm's length from the kayak and parallel to where he or she is sitting. Drawing the paddle toward the kayak causes the boat to move sideways, or side-step, toward the paddle.

Although paddling strokes give a kayaker better control of the boat, there are still times when the kayak will tip over. In these instances, it is vital for the kayaker to know how to perform either a wet exit or an Eskimo roll. The wet exit allows a paddler to get out of the kayak if it capsizes. If a paddler is wearing a spray skirt, this safety technique is essential to prevent becoming trapped in the boat underwater. To perform this move, a kayaker reaches forward and releases the spray skirt from the cockpit. Then the kayaker pushes on the sides of the cockpit to propel his or her body out and away from the boat, and he or she swims to the surface.

To increase stability, some kayaks feature pedal-like foot rests in the front that a kayaker can press his or her feet against. These pedals aid a kayaker in balancing and help to prevent unnecessary motion in a kayak.

When beginning kayaking, learning the necessary skills from an expert will give a novice kayaker an advantage in the water. Learning with a group can provide a kayaker with a support system in case of difficulties.

As opposed to the wet exit, which is an escape technique, the Eskimo roll is a motion used to right the kayak if it tips over. In an Eskimo roll, the kayaker never leaves the boat or detaches the spray skirt. When a kayak capsizes and the kayaker is upside down underwater, the Eskimo roll is performed by pushing the paddle away from the kayak toward the bottom of the lake or river and simultaneously snapping the hips up toward the sky. These actions work together to right the kayak.

Besides knowing how to control the kayak, paddlers who embark on group adventures must know standard kayaking signals, which help group members communicate when they are far apart and unable to hear one another. Often, leaders or guides will run rapids first and relay information back to the group by holding the paddle over their head in different positions. If a waterway splits or is not easy to follow, holding the paddle at a 45-degree angle to the right signals for others to stay to the right, while holding it at a 45-degree angle to the left means to stay left. In order to get paddlers to stop—due to a dangerous area ahead or for a brief rest—the paddle is held parallel to the ground with both hands. If the paddle is held perpendicular to the ground, it means all clear, and kayakers may proceed forward with limited caution. A paddle held perpendicular to the ground and waving to the right and then the left means there is an immediate emergency. In such a situation, group members usually have been previously informed of their individual responsibilities. For instance, one person may be designated to call for help, while others may be responsible for boiling water for hot drinks in case hypothermia is an issue.

The Eskimo roll had been practiced by kayakers for years, but in 1927, Hans Eduard Pawlatta, a member of the Vienna Kayak Club, perfected the roll technique. The Eskimo-Pawlatta roll allowed paddlers to resurface in their kayaks, unlike the earliest Eskimo roll, which was used primarily for escape.

Water Ratings

Pounding rapids and rolling surf can—and should—intimidate beginning kayakers, while advanced kayakers may look at such water with a gleam of anticipation. In order to prevent serious accidents, kayakers must know both their own skill level and the difficulty level of any body of water they want to paddle. Since at least 1959, river rapids have been rated according to a six-class scale, with Class I rapids being the easiest and Class VI the hardest. Most white-water guidebooks, as well as the Web site of the American Whitewater Association, list the ratings of various rivers.

Class I rapids consist of fast-moving water with ripples, small waves, and few obstructions, making them easy for even beginning kayakers to negotiate. Performing a wet exit or Eskimo roll on such rapids is relatively easy, so the risk in running them is small.

Class II rapids have wide, clear chutes that trained kayakers can easily navigate. The rocks and small to medium-sized waves of these rapids can be avoided even with little to no scouting. Rapids at the more difficult end of this classification are designated Class II+.

Class III rapids contain moderate, irregular waves that cannot be avoided. These rapids can easily swamp a kayak. Good boat control in tight passages or around ledges may be required, and large waves or complex current caused by downed trees may be present but can be avoided. Scouting is essential, especially for inexperienced paddlers. Rapids at the easier and more difficult ends of this classification are designated Class III- and Class III+ respectively.

Class IV waterways are advanced and powerful, requiring expert boat handling in turbulent water. These rapids may have large, unavoidable waves and holes or small, tight chutes requiring fast maneuvers. Kayakers may have to execute quick, reliable turns in order to pause for a moment to scout rapids or to rest. Scouting is absolutely essential, and a wet exit or Eskimo roll may be difficult to perform due to the speed of the water or obstacles such as rocks and downed trees lying below the surface. As a result, group assistance or an excellent Eskimo roll are essential for rescue or to right a capsized boat. Rapids at the lower and upper ends of this class range are designated Class IV- and Class IV+ respectively.

Class V rapids are for experts only, since they are extremely long and obstructed, and can be very violent. Drops may contain unavoidable waves and holes or steep, congested chutes with complex, demanding routes. These rapids can create big waves that cover long sections of river, demanding a high level of fitness. The few eddies that do exist in such rapids may be small, turbulent, or difficult to reach. Scouting is recommended but may be difficult due to rough terrain or obstacles. Rescues out of this type of water are dangerous and difficult, even for experts. Class V is an open-ended, multiple-level scale designated by Class V.0, V.1, V.2, and so on; each of these levels progresses in difficulty.

Class VI rapids are extreme and often deadly. These rapids have almost never been attempted, even by the most skilled kayakers. Errors, such as capsizing the kayak or misjudging the position of obstacles in the water, may result in death or severe injury, and rescue may be impossible.

Challenges that lie around river bends add to a kayaker's sense of anticipation. Still, scouting a river before kayaking is a critical precaution. Attempting new watercourses can be dangerous, especially to novice kayakers.

Although rapid ratings certainly help kayakers determine whether or not their skill level is sufficient for a particular rapid, they cannot be relied upon alone. Rapids are subject to change; for instance, high water levels might completely submerge a rapid and turn it into simply swift-moving water, while low water levels might turn an easy rapid into a dangerous one with huge boulders protruding from the surface of the water. In addition, rivers change from year to year, and new obstacles such as fallen trees can affect the current flow and velocity of the water. For these reasons, and because ratings can differ between rapids on the same river, kayakers must scout each rapid before attempting to kayak it.

Of course, not only white-water kayakers need to be prepared for water conditions. Open-water kayakers must also research each body of water before dipping their boat into it. Unlike white water, open water has no rating system, as conditions can vary from day to day—or even hour to hour—due to many environmental factors, including wind, tide, temperature, season, and recent rains. One day a lake might be warm and calm, without a ripple on the water, and the next, cold and windy with big, pounding waves. Thus, kayakers must monitor the water, know how tides change, and be alert for changing wind levels.

Lakes, rivers, and oceans across the globe offer kayakers an opportunity to explore. For adventure-seekers searching out white water, there are fast-moving rivers all over the world that provide a variety of challenges from Class I to Class V rapids. The New River Gorge in West Virginia provides 53 miles (85 km) of river, with rapids ranging from Class I to Class V. The variety of paddling available on this river makes it an excellent choice for paddlers of all abilities. Another exceptional white-water river is the Colorado, which flows 1,400 miles (2,250 km) from the Rocky Mountains of Colorado

A kayak is a fantastic way to explore rivers or lakes in an unfamiliar place. Traveling various watercourses, such as the Haruru Falls on the Waitangi River in New Zealand, can take tourists to locations that are otherwise inaccessible.

through Arizona and offers Class I to Class IV rapids. This mighty river runs through the Grand Canyon, providing an awesome adventure—and amazing scenery—for kayakers.

Flat-water kayaking, although a bit more relaxing than white-water kayaking, is great exercise and allows for the exploration of remote areas. The Boundary Waters Canoe Area (BWCA) in Northeastern Minnesota and the Quetico Provincial Park (QPP) in southern Ontario, Canada, which share a boundary line, offer some of the best wilderness kayaking in North America. The BWCA and QPP prohibit motorized boats on their waterways, which helps maintain a true wilderness experience. Paddling this area takes kayakers away from modern luxuries back in time across lakes connected by portages forged by French voyageurs during the fur trade era of the late 1700s.

The Apostle Islands off the coast of Lake Superior in northern Wisconsin are also fairly remote but provide paddlers with a different type of flat-water experience from the BWCA and QPP. Lake Superior's vastness makes paddlers feel almost as if they are on the ocean, with water stretching beyond the horizon. Since the lake's lapping surf can quickly grow in size to brutal breaking waves that present substantial dangers to inexperienced paddlers, kayaking here requires not only excellent paddling skills, but also the ability to perform wet exits, Eskimo rolls, and medical safety skills in the case of an emergency.

The northeastern portion of the U.S. also provides excellent kayaking locations throughout the Adirondack Mountain Range. These peaks hold a wealth of lakes and rivers for flat-water and white-water paddlers alike. Unfortunately for a solace-seeking kayaker, many of these bodies of water are crowded with paddlers, motorized boats, jet skis, and large numbers of tourists. Despite these sources of unwanted noise, the Adirondack's lakes and rivers are great locations for multi- or single-day paddling excursions.

Kayaking competitions often take place on man-made rivers and lakes where fast-flowing water and tricky obstacles can be closely monitored for safety. The first man-made slalom rapids course was built for the Munich Olympic Games in 1972.

Kayaking Competitions and Festivals

In 1987, at the age of 10, Rebecca Giddens of Green Bay, Wisconsin, started kayaking at a YMCA canoe camp. She quickly fell in love with the sport and committed herself to it, training daily by lifting weights, completing short- and long-distance water workouts, and cross-training by roller blading, hiking, biking, and surfing. Seventeen years later, Giddens's dedication paid off when she placed second in the K1 slalom event at the 2004 Olympics in Athens, Greece.

Kayaking has been an official Olympic sport since 1936, when men's flat-water racing was introduced to the Olympic games. Today, Olympic competitors vie for gold in several flat-water and slalom events, featuring K1, K2, K4, C1, and C2 boats. The letters "K" and "C" indicate a kayak and canoe respectively, and the number indicates how many people fit into the boat. Although C1 and C2 kayaks are technically called canoes, they are almost structurally identical to kayaks, except that they must be at least one and a half feet (0.5 m) wider than a kayak. In addition, C1 and C2 paddlers use a single-bladed paddle, while other kayakers use a double-bladed paddle.

Today, there are four categories of slalom races in the Olympics—men's K1, C1, and C2, and women's K1. Slalom races require paddlers to maneuver their boats down white water through a series of color-coded gates. Kayakers

Marathon flat-water competitions vary in length and type of watercourse raced. Rough water racing includes obstacles in stretches of rivers, while flat-water racing competitions are held on lakes, rivers, canals, and open seawater. Flat-water marathon races can be 5 miles (8 km) to 125 miles (201 km) in length.

pass through green and white gates on their way downstream. But to pass through red and white gates, they must turn their boat upstream and run against the current. For every gate touched, two seconds are added to the paddler's time, while a missed gate results in a 50-second time penalty. Each kayaker runs the course twice, and the winner is determined by the fastest cumulative time after penalties for touching or missing gates are added. The slalom event at the 2004 Olympics featured 20 gates along a 270-meter (295 yd.) man-made white-water river. Benoit Peschier of France raced through the K1 slalom in a total time of 187.96 seconds to take the men's gold, while Elena Kaliska of Slovakia won the women's K1 slalom, coming in just 4.59 seconds ahead of Giddens with a total time of 210.03 seconds. Kayakers from France and Slovakia won gold in the men's C1 and C2 events respectively.

In addition to the 4 slalom events, the 2004 Olympics also featured 12 flat-water races. Men's events included the 500-meter (550 yd.) K1, K2, C1, and C2 races, as well as the 1,000-meter (1,090 yd.) K1, K2, K4, C1, and C2 races, while women competed in the 500-meter (550 yd.) K1, K2, and K4 events. In each of the races, paddlers rowed in heats across an 11.5-foot-deep (3.5 m) lake, with the top nine finishers racing in the events' finals. Individual paddlers and teams from Germany did especially well in the flat-water events, earning four gold and three silver medals for their country.

Although the Olympics are the most elite kayaking competition, they are certainly not the only one. Both flat-water and slalom races are held on lakes, rivers, and artificial waterways around the world. In addition, new types of kayak races that aren't recognized as Olympic sports have been developed. Wild-water racing, for example, involves racing down a three- to five-mile (4.8–8 km) stretch of Class III to IV river rapids. With a World Championship race attended by athletes from more than 40 nations, this sport is growing in popularity and is considered by some to be the purest form of kayaking. As guidebook author Fletcher Anderson says, "Wild-water racing is pure white-water paddling, often called the race of truth. Some 20 minutes after leaving the start, the racer arrives at the finish line. In between is the river in its natural state and nothing else."

Freestyle kayaking is the most recent development in the sport of kayaking and entails performing maneuvers and tricks on white water. Popular tricks include cartwheels, in which the kayak appears to cartwheel through the water, with first the bow and then the stern dipping underwater; split wheels, in which the kayak is spun while standing vertically in the water; and blunts, in which the entire kayak pops out of the water.

Wild-water racing takes an immense amount of skill and courage since the course being run is often unknown to competitors. Paddlers typically ride 4 to 5 miles (7–8 km) of class III to IV whitewater rapids. These competitions are extremely challenging—even for expert kayakers.

Racing is a great way to increase the public's awareness of kayaking. Kayakers who partici-

pate in competitions usually are members of a kayaking or paddling club. Some kayaking

outfitters or clubs will host races or festivals so the public can learn about the sport.

Kayaking continues to grow as an adventure sport for competitors, thrill seekers, and leisure lovers. Whether traveling to unknown watercourses to ride rapids, or drifting on a familiar lake or river, practice and preparedness are critical for an enjoyable ride.

The incredible loop trick involves flipping the kayak in the water—much like a somersault. Judges rate freestyle kayakers on both the difficulty of the tricks they perform and the amount of control they demonstrate over their kayak.

Kayak festivals offer competitions and more, providing everyone from the novice to the expert with the opportunity to learn about kayaking through seminars, lectures, equipment demonstrations, and instructional training. One of the largest kayak festivals is the Ashlu River Festival in British Columbia, Canada, which hosts more than 200 participants from around the world and includes kayak clinics, product demonstrations, seminars, guided trips down nearby rivers, and instruction from expert guides.

A popular open-water festival is held in Two Harbors, Minnesota, every August. This festival is geared toward families and includes kid-friendly instruction, as well as short races for kids. To get adults involved, there are clinics and seminars, as well as several longer races.

A festival catering to the more extreme side of the sport is the Santa Cruz Kayak Surf Festival, near Santa Cruz, California. Held in March, this festival features a surf kayak competition that attracts some of the best surf kayakers in the world. Participants paddle their kayaks atop the crest of a wave—much like surfers ride waves—while attempting to make various acrobatic moves, including rolls, cartwheels, and loops, for a panel of judges.

Surf kayaking is an excellent example of how kayaking continues to evolve today. More advanced materials are being developed, allowing kayakers to create new and innovative paddling, surfing, and maneuvering skills. Competitions and festivals also continue to grow and change as kayaking becomes more affordable and accessible to the public. Newer, lighter kayaks mean that it is easier for paddlers of all ages to carry their boats across portages and experience places that were once inaccessible. As the sport continues to advance and grow, the draw of big white water or remote lakes will continue to call kayakers worldwide to begin wild adventures.

RECOMMENDED READING

Ferrero, Franco, ed. *Canoe and Kayak Handbook*. Bangor, UK: Pesda Press, 2002.

Foster, Nigel. *Nigel Foster's Sea Kayaking*. Old Saybrook, Conn.: Globe Pequot Press, 1997.

Heacox, Kim. *The Only Kayak: Journeys Into the Heart of Alaska*. New York: Lyons Press, 2005.

Krazuer, Steven M. *Kayaking: Whitewater and Touring Basics*. New York: W.W. Norton, 1995.

U'Ren, Stephen, B. *Performance Kayaking*. Harrisburg, Penn.: Stackpole Books, 1990.

WEB SITES OF INTEREST

www.americanwhitewater.org
Web site of the American Whitewater Association. Explains the rating system for rapids and lists ratings of various rivers throughout the U.S.

http://www.daveyhearn.com
Provides links and information on white-water and slalom racing, as well as information on professional kayakers, including Rebecca Giddens.

http://www.kayakfestival.org
Home of the Two Harbors kayak festival.

http://www.seakayak.ws/kayak/kayak.nsf/NavigationList/NT00005696
Provides explanations and pictures of different types of kayaks.

http://www.wetdawg.com/pages/tour_tips_display.php?t=70&c=16
Names and defines the various features of a river, including eddies, undercuts, and boils.

http://www.whitewater.org/squish/ashlu/ashlu_festival.htm
Provides information on the Ashlu River Festival and gives details about specific activities during the four-day event.

http://www.uscg.mil/hq/gm/mse4/pfdseldata.htm
Describes how to choose the proper flotation device for various water activities.

http://www.usack.org
Highlights the U.S. Olympic Canoe and Kayak team, and provides information on various kayak disciplines, governance of races, and more.

GLOSSARY

bow—the front section of a boat

chutes—narrow, constricted portions of a river

cockpits—openings in kayaks in which paddlers sit

drops—places in rapids where the kayak leaves the water as it drops from an elevated section to a lower section; often caused by rocks or large boulders

dry suit—a suit made of rubberized latex that keeps paddlers warm and dry

eddies—places where the water moves in a different direction or speed than the main current; eddies are often used by paddlers to rest without being carried by the current

flat water—rivers and lakes that have no white water (rapids) and very little, if any, current

holes—dips in the water caused by drops off rocks, boulders, or other obstacles; holes can suck a kayak in and trap it

hypalon—a synthetic rubber used to build kayaks; its formal name is chlorosulfonated polyethylene

Kevlar—a lightweight fiberglass and resin material used to make kayaks and paddles

latex—a synthetic rubber used for clothing, balloons, and medical gloves

open water—an ocean or large lake that is exposed to winds, tides, currents, and other extreme and constantly changing weather conditions

portages—short trails that connect waterways and require paddlers to carry their kayaks and gear from one body of water to the next

PVC—abbreviation for polyvinyl chloride, which is used for electrical insulation, films, and pipes, as well as the construction of kayaks

rescue bags—small nylon bags with a hole in the bottom to which a rope is attached; the rope coils inside the bag and can be thrown to a swimmer who needs assistance

rocker—the amount of curve on the bottom of a kayak from the bow to the stern

rudder—a movable, thin piece of plastic at or near the stern to control the direction the kayak moves

scouting—examining a waterway from land or water for hazards and dangers

stern—the rear end of a boat

touring—using a kayak to tour or explore an area

voyageurs—French fur traders of the 1700s who trapped and traded along the U.S.-Canada border

wet suit—tight-fitting neoprene clothing that keeps one warm when immersed in cold water

white-water—describes frothy water that is often found in rapids and has a white appearance

INDEX